ARE WE GOING TO MISS CHRISTMAS?

ARE WE GOING TO MISS CHRISTMAS?

BY

DOROTHY J. KOZAR

CO-AUTHORS

EMERY, HARPER AND PAISLEY

~

ILLUSTRATIONS BY MADELYN GRAHAM

VOL 1 OF SERIES:
"NOTHING MISSING, NOTHING BROKEN"

XULON PRESS

Xulon Press
2301 Lucien Way #415
Maitland, FL 32751
407.339.4217
www.xulonpress.com

© 2021 by Dorothy J. Kozar

Unless otherwise indicated,Scripture quotations taken from the
King James Version (KJV) – *public domain*

Paperback ISBN-13: 978-1-6628-3090-7
Hard Cover ISBN-13: 978-1-6628-3091-4

DEDICATION

Special thanks goes to Calvin Gilmore Productions. Not only do they entertain, but are also known for their humanitarian contributions. Thank you Jordan for believing in our book and helping empower the young writers and the emerging artist.

The Carolina Opry Theater is extraordinarily superb! The show's variety is the largest we have ever seen. It is sure to please every taste. All the actors, comedians, dancers, musicians and singers are extremely talented professionals. They express their hearts in all they do. All the staff invites the audience in and makes everyone feel like friends and family.

Various shows run throughout each year. We have never been disappointed. We go there when life has been too busy and we always leave refreshed. Their annual Christmas Show is over-the-top awesome! The entire auditorium erupts with awe, wonder and applause. We recommend that you experience the best of the best. You can visit them at 8901 North Kings Highway, Myrtle Beach, SC 29572 https://thecarolinaopry.com/

Gratitude and honor goes to Charlie Shamp, President of Destiny Encounters who exhorted me to continue writing.

We dedicate this book to children of all ages. Most of all, our devotion and praise goes to the one lifted up on its last few pages

Three sisters are riding in the car with Grandpa and Grandma. They are giggling and excited to be going to the beach! Suddenly, Emery stops laughing and shouts; "Are we going to miss Christmas?"

$\mathcal{E}$mery is thinking about her parents at home alone.

It is December. She wonders if they will have Christmas without her. Emery did not want to miss it. No one does!

1

---
[1] Photo by Lynda Hinton

With eyes wide open, Harper looks at Emery! "What?"

Now, *all* the sisters are wondering if they really are going to miss Christmas!

Quickly, Grandma said; "No! Of course not! You will not miss Christmas! Why would you think that?" She explains; "We will only be away for three days. Christmas is not until next week." Emery took a deep breath and smiled. Everyone is happy again.

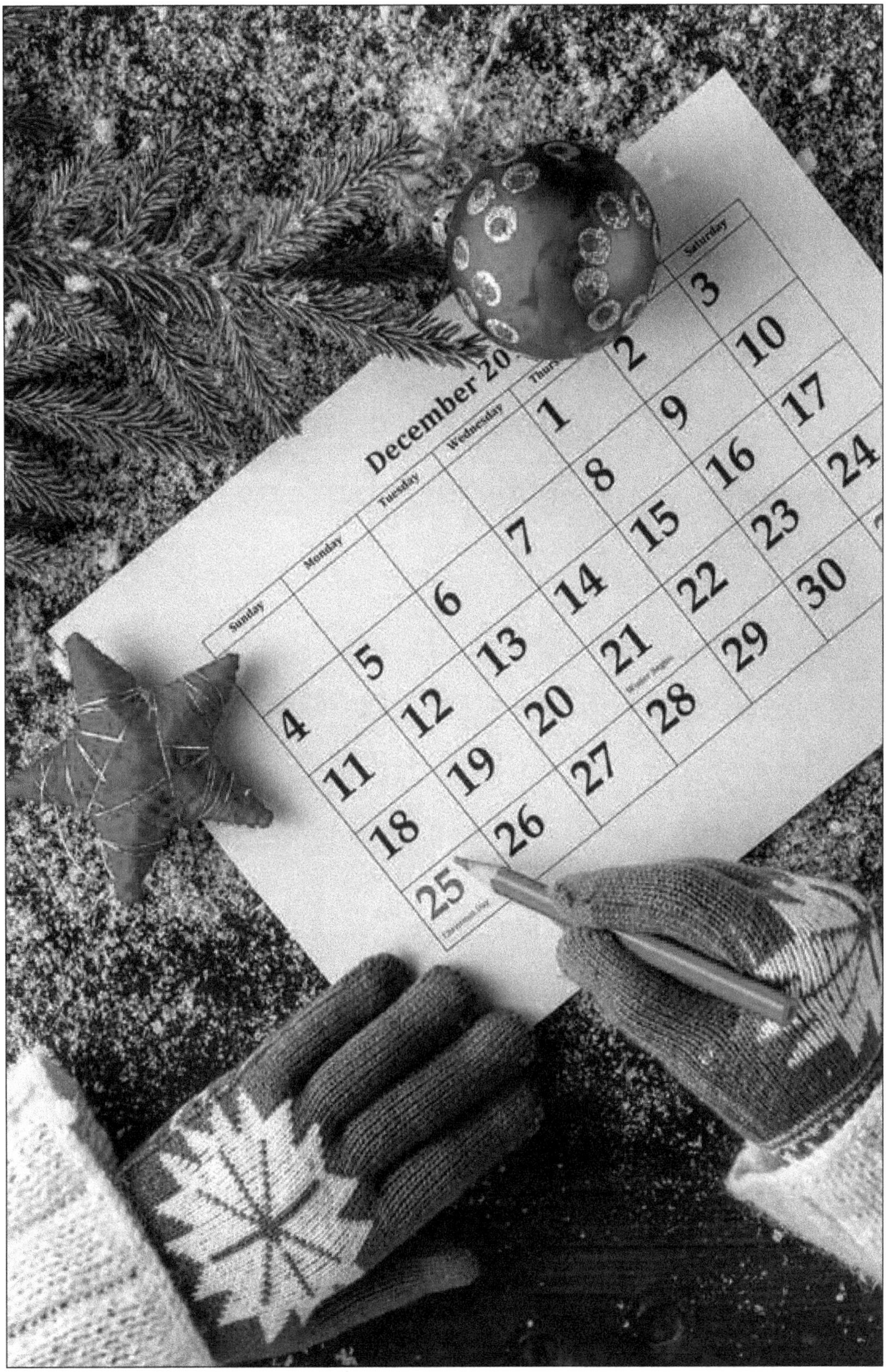
December
Sunday
Monday
Tuesday
Wednesday
Saturday
1 2 3 4 5 6 7 8 9 10 11 12 13 14 15 16 17 18 19 20 21 22 23 24 25 26 27 28 29 30

inally, we are at the beach hotel. Bouncing around and stretching our legs, we start unpacking. Then we settle in to relax.

Suddenly, Grandpa said;
"Oh no, I forgot to pack my toothbrush! Girls, you can play a little longer; then put on your pretty dresses. We're going to the toothbrush store."

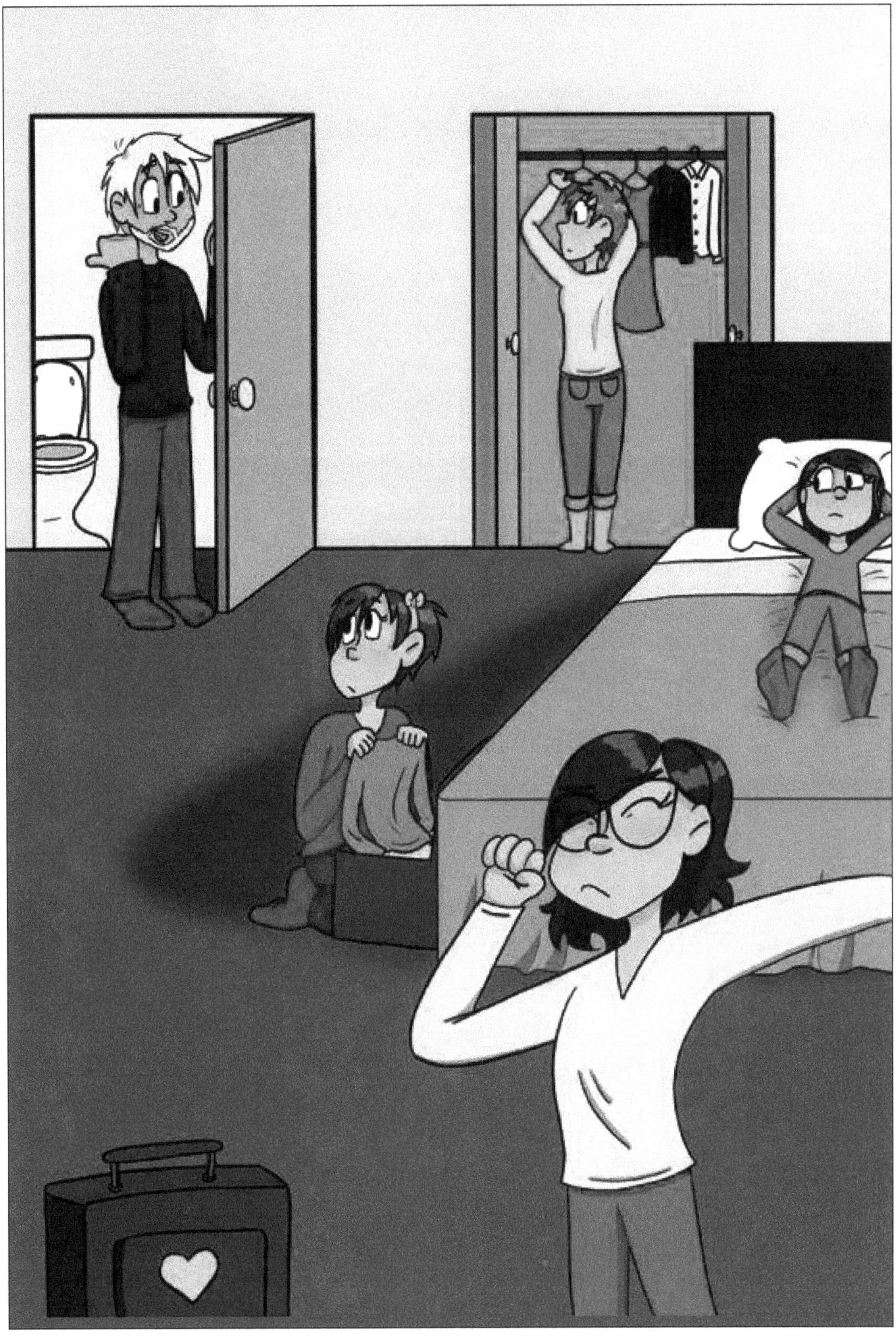

$\mathcal{E}$veryone is in the car again. Harper whispers to Emery;
"Why are we wearing nice dresses to the toothbrush store?"

Just then, Paisley shouted; "Grandpa! You missed the store!" Grandpa didn't seem to hear and kept on driving. Then he turned and parked in front of this big special building.

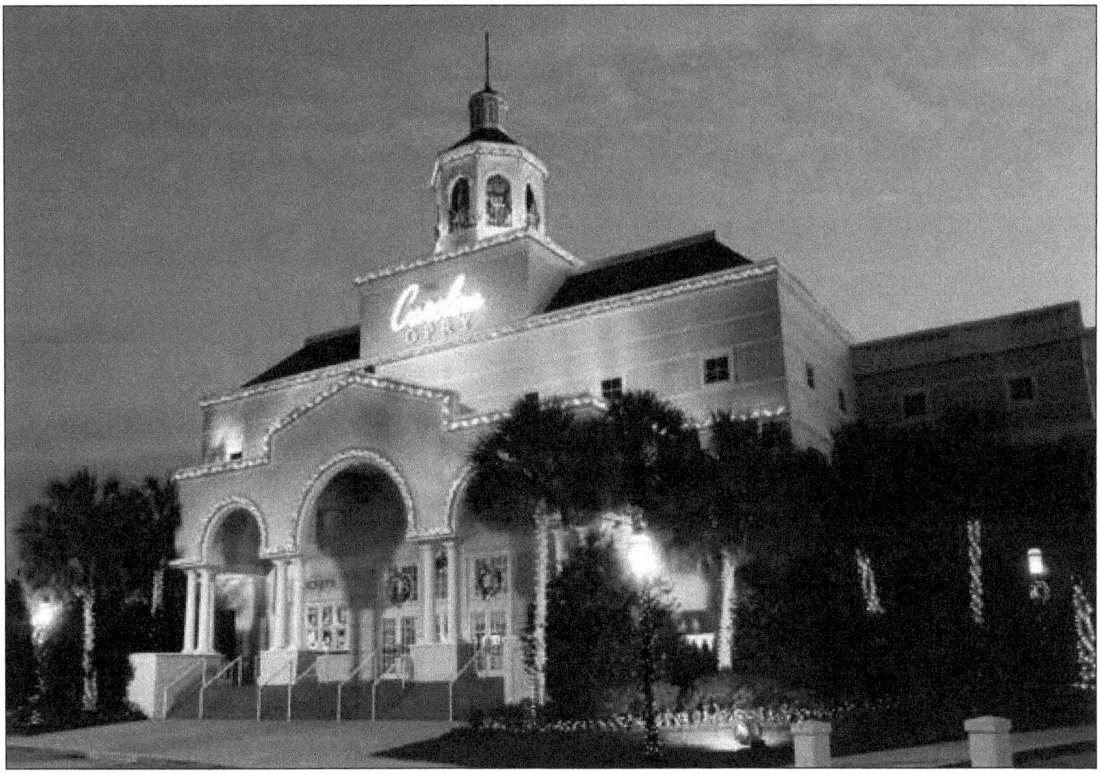

2

² Photo by Jordan Watkins: The Carolina Opry

We scramble out of the car. "Where are we?" Grandma leads us up the steps. The big doors open.

WOW! Surprise! We jump for joy!

Look! There's Santa!

3

---

3 Photos by Jordan Watkins: The Carolina Opry

$\mathcal{E}$mery is squealing with delight!

We see Christmas trees along the stairs.

Glittery stripes and colored lights!

Sparkly ornaments everywhere!

Candy canes are placed with care.

Christmas! Christmas! Everywhere!

4

⁴ Photos by Jordan Watkins: The Carolina Opry

Next, we see a giant auditorium and a beautiful stage!

We are wiggly in our seats and in our feet!

The lights go dim and the show begins.

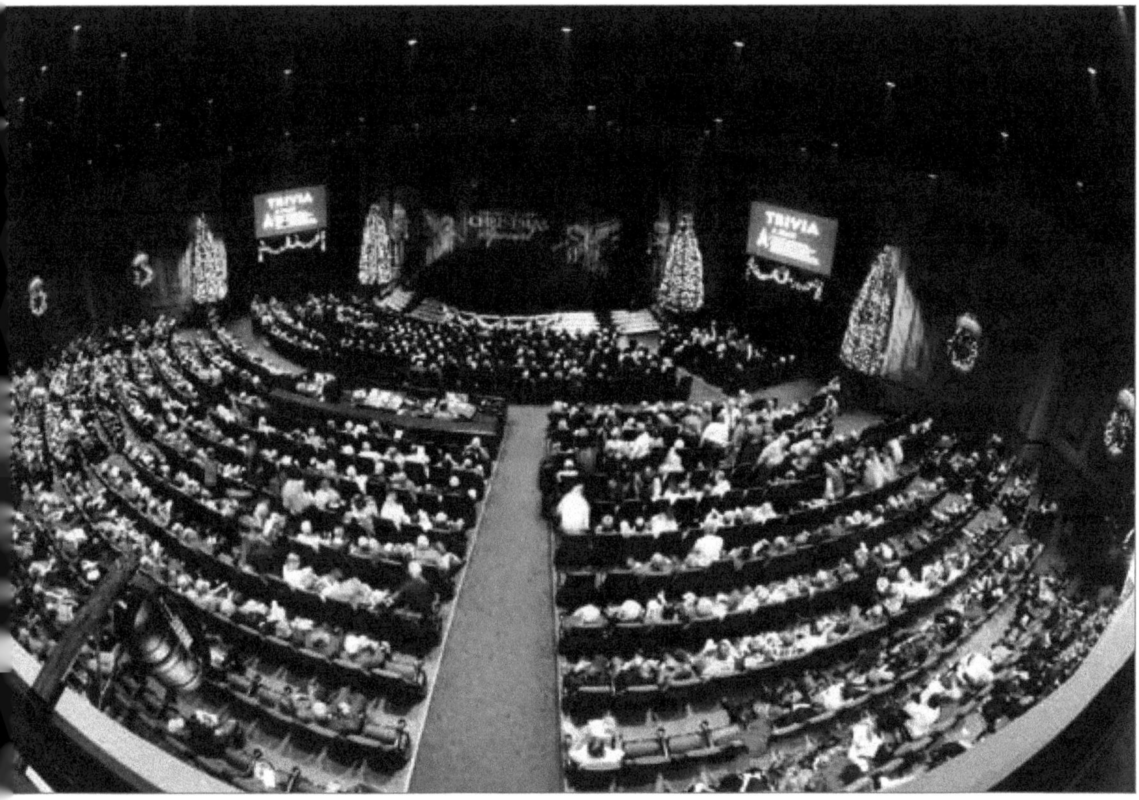

5

---

[5] Photo by Jordan Watkins: The Carolina Opry

There is singing and dancing. The costumes are brilliant Christmas colors. Look! There comes a real horse and sleigh! It's a snowy scene, which makes our day!

6

---
6 Photo by Jordan Watkins: The Carolina Opry

"All kids, please come up here on the stage!", says the Elf.

We climb up the steps to be in the show! The spot lights are dancing with us! We sing Jingle Bells. Then, we clap our hands and run back to our seats. "Thank you, Grandpa, for the big surprise!"

7

7 Photo by Jordan Watkins: The Carolina Opry

$\mathcal{E}$mery is the first to fall asleep on the ride home.

Harper and Paisley finally see their neighborhood.

Dad is shoveling snow off their driveway.

We ran to hug him! Emery wakes up and rubs her eyes. Seeing her Dad, she smiles and shouts; "Did you miss us?"

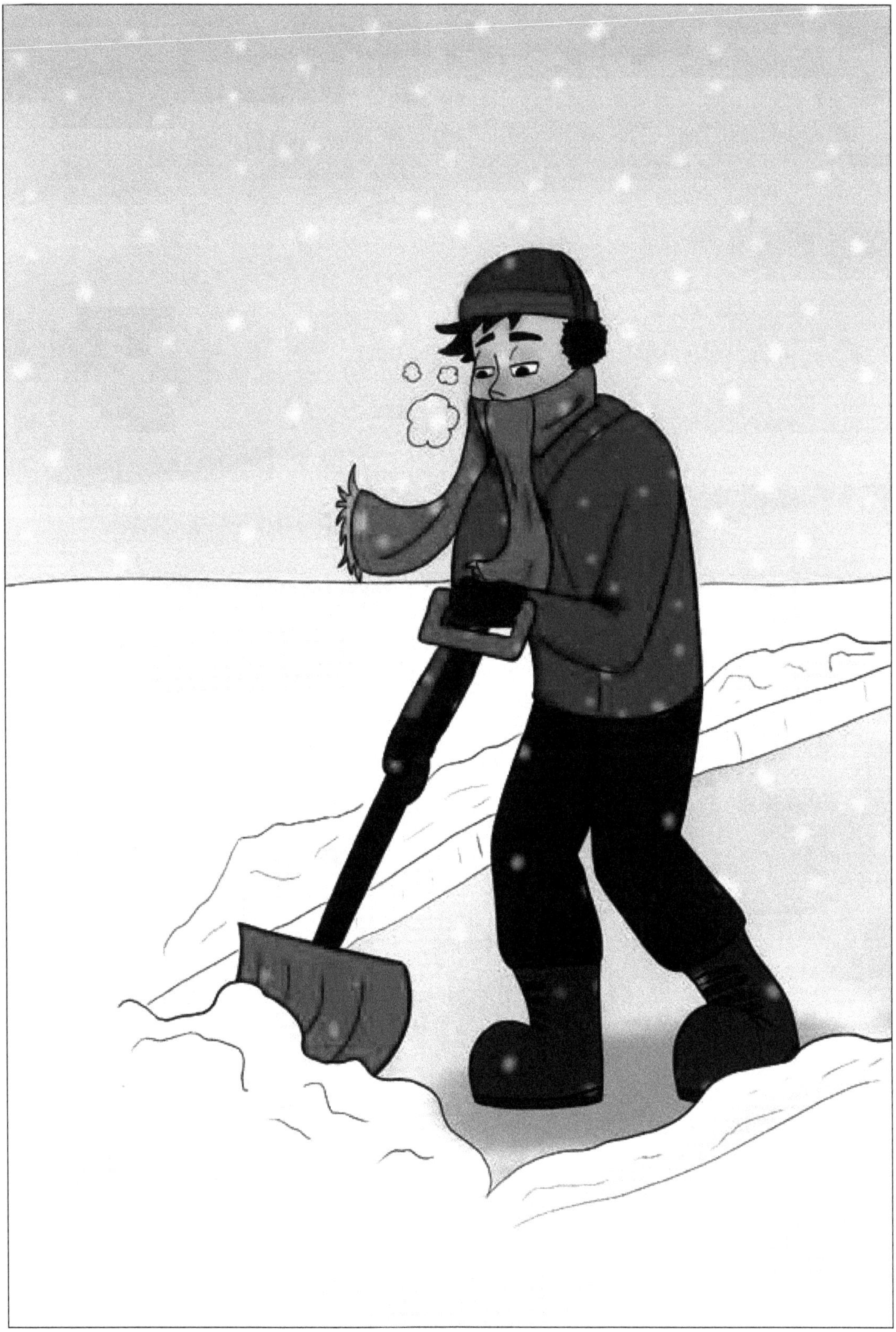

Emery and her sisters have been keeping a close watch on the calendar. Look! Christmas Eve is here!

The girls, their parents, all the cousins, aunts and uncles go to Grandma and Grandpa's house for a Christmas Eve celebration!

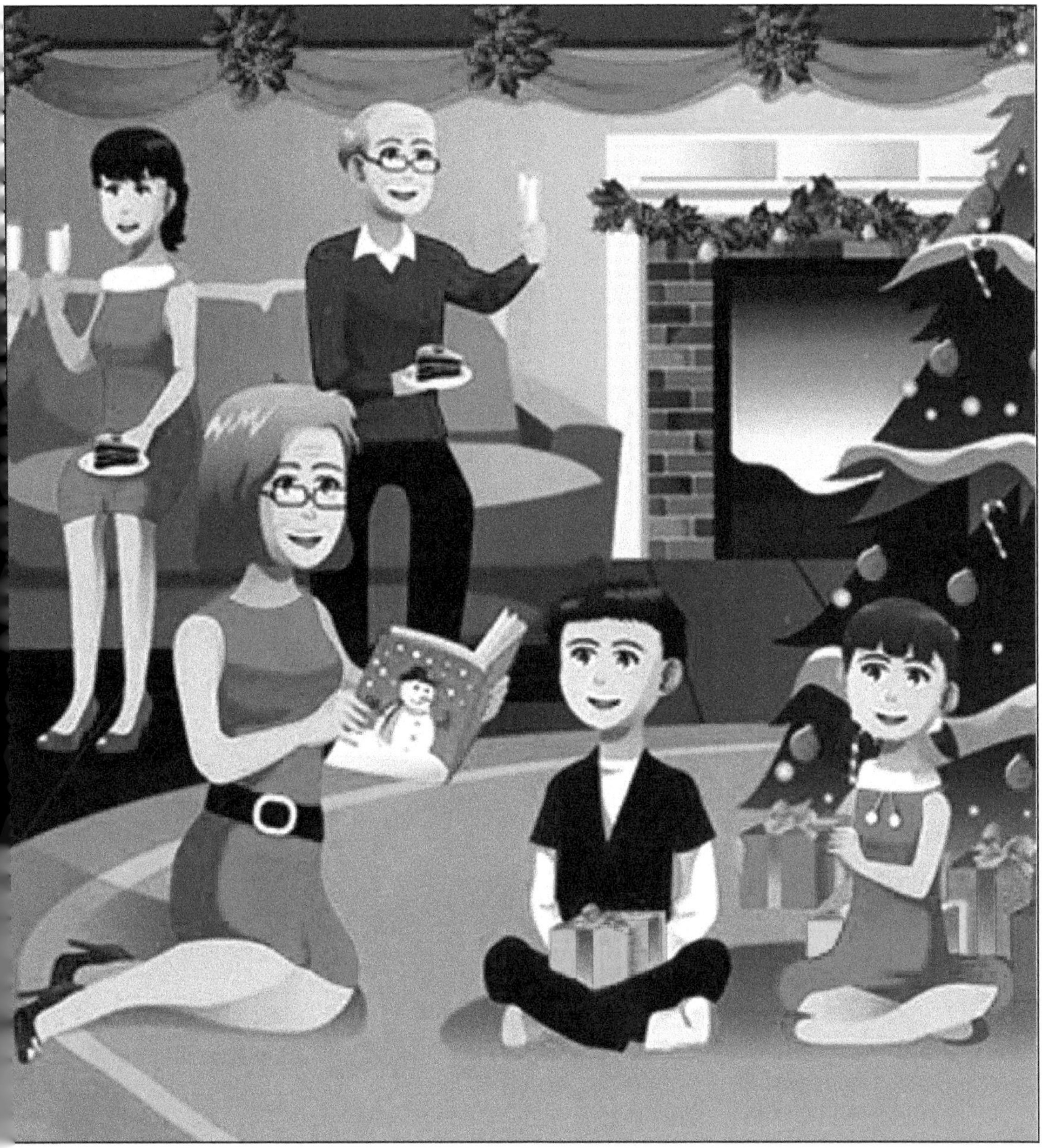

Emery woke up the next morning at her home. She rubbed her sleepy eyes and ran down stairs. Sliding in, wearing candy cane socks, she saw her family by the Christmas tree.

Her sisters squealed with laughter and love! Emery said; "We did NOT miss Christmas!"

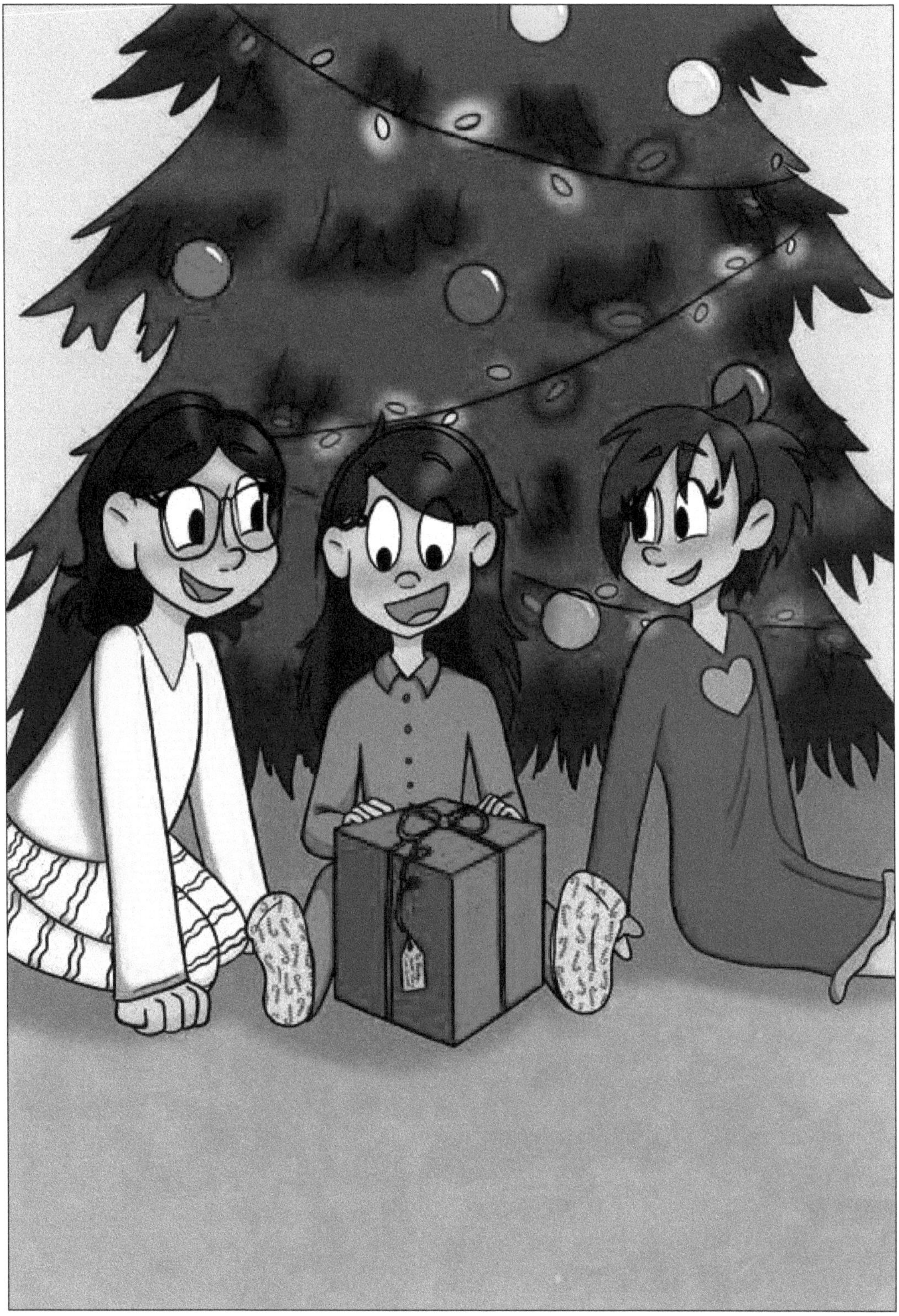

We don't want YOU to miss the BEST gift.

We don't want you to miss the BEST love.

Over two thousand years ago, a very big surprise was coming, but some people missed it because they were not looking for it.

However, other people watched and waited with great excitement!

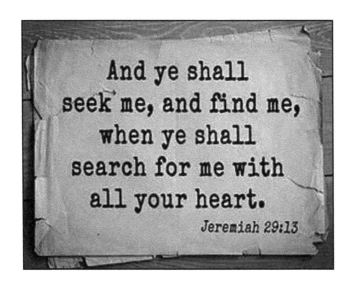

And ye shall
seek me, and find me,
when ye shall
search for me with
all your heart.

Jeremiah 29:13

hen one night, a special bright star appeared in the sky! A brilliant show of God's glory came with many angels singing and celebrating:

♦

"And the angel said unto them, Fear not: for, behold, I bring you good tidings of great joy, which shall be to all people. For unto you is born this day in the city of David a Saviour, which is Christ the Lord. And this shall be a sign unto you; Ye shall find the babe wrapped in swaddling clothes, lying in a manger. And suddenly there was with the angel a multitude of the heavenly host praising God, and saying, Glory to God in the highest and on earth peace, good will toward men." (Luke 2:10-14, KJV, *Olive Tree Bible Study App.*)

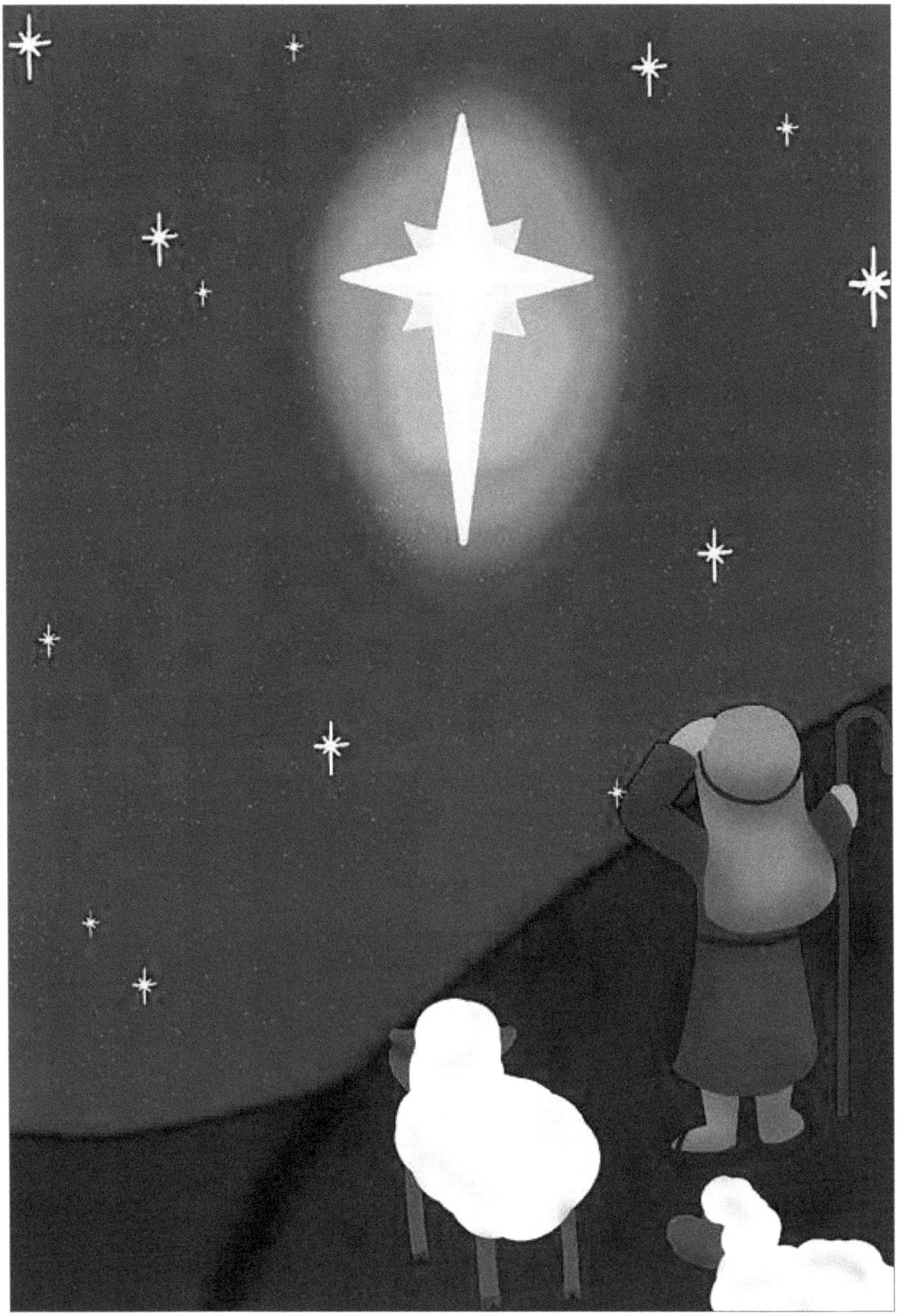

Baby Jesus would soon grow.

He was loving and obedient.

He fixed what was broken!

He completes what is missing!

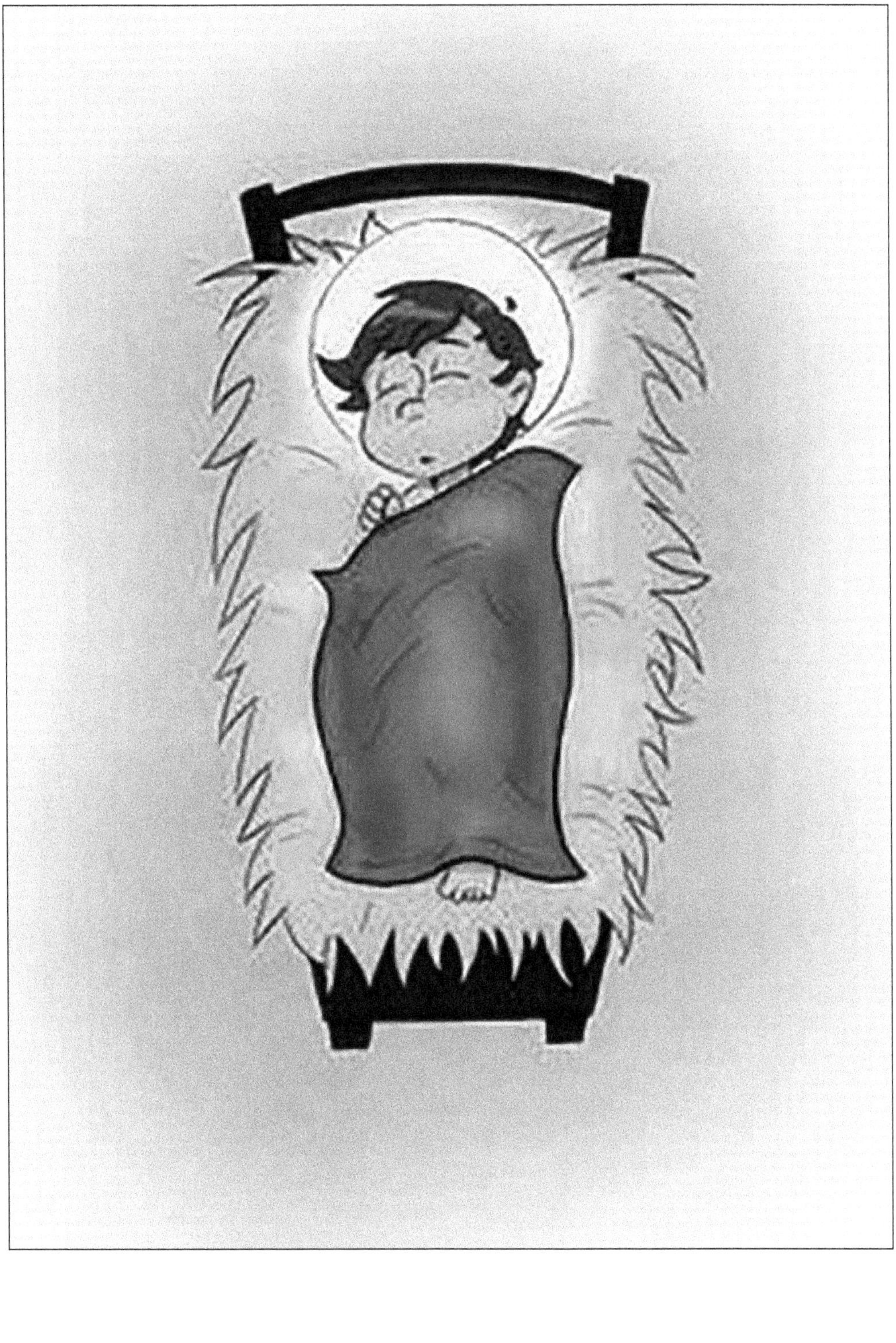

We don't want YOU to miss Jesus!

He is Christ the Lord! Son of the living God.

He has a big love for you.

He helps us every day and night.

Ask for him. Call his name. He is near.

When we choose Jesus, we can live
with him forever.

The Holy Bible is a book all about Jesus.

He is alive and he is coming again!

Believe. Be ready. Be excited!

Are you going to miss Jesus?

No! Of course not!

Go find him!

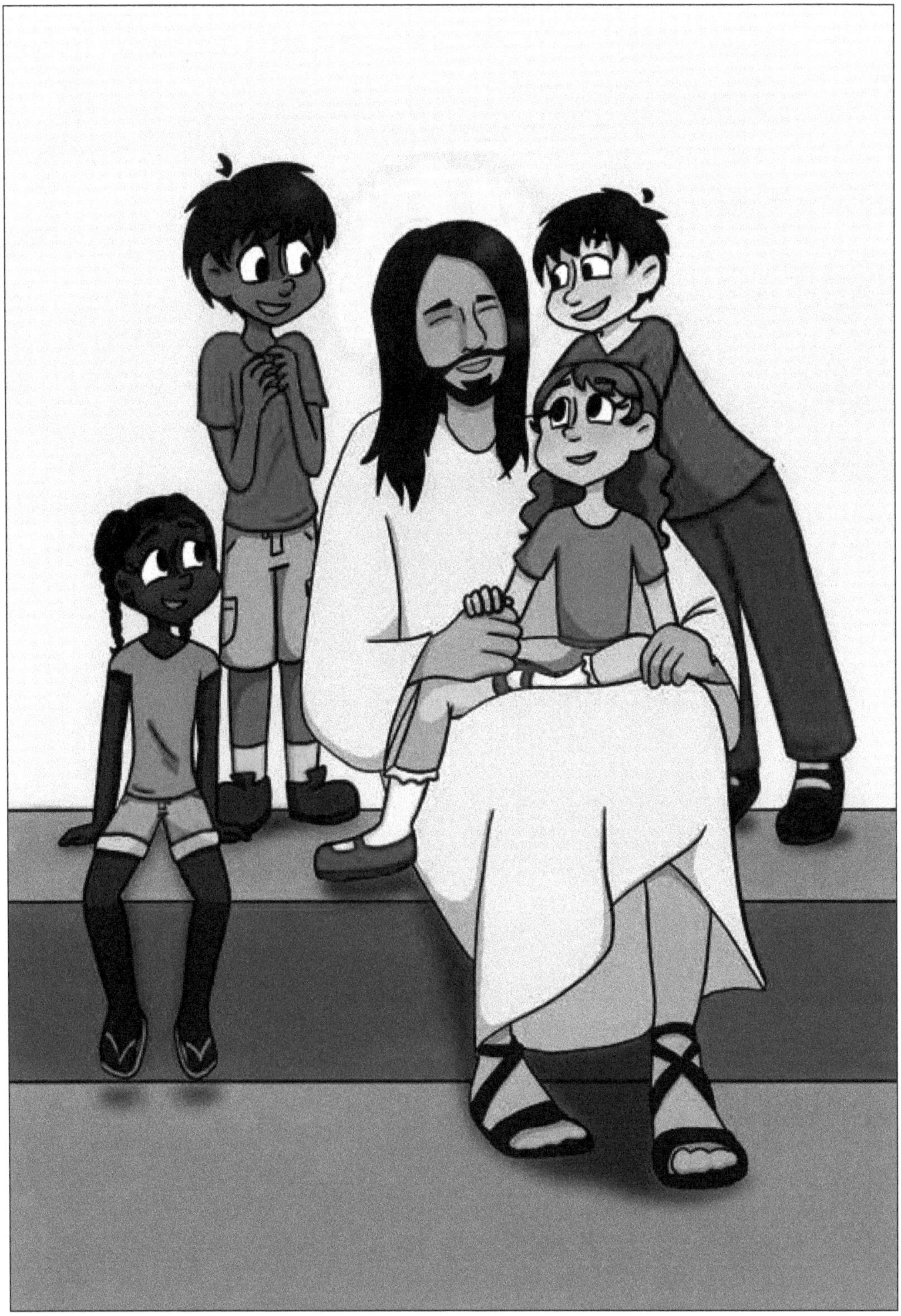

REFERENCES

Harper Collins Christian Publishing, Inc. *Olive Tree Bible Study App* Version 6.0.14 Holy Bible, KJV App updated January 8, 2018 https://itunes.apple.com/app/id332615624?8&referrer=-click%3D96a93bae-2851400d-ab13-c48a06ab859f

Graham, Madelyn of Ohio, *Illustrations including cover art.* Instagram @drawing_with_madz

Hinton, Lynda, Photography f1, - unsplash, lynda-hinton-RpWCPDxMcSo-unsplash.jpg

Watkins, Jordan, Vice President, Director of Marketing, *Gilmore Entertainment,* Photography, *ff* 2-7 jwatkins@GilmoreEntertainment.com

ABOUT THE AUTHOR

Dorothy Kozar is an author, public speaker and ordained minister living in North Carolina. She received a masters degree from Duke University. She retired after thirty years as a Nurse Practitioner. She writes children and adult books to equip, inspire and empower. As a mother and grandmother, she brings the following generations into a literary legacy: https://literarylegacy.org Dorothy is available as keynote speaker against domestic violence and other topics. She and her husband, Steve, are lead ministers at "House of Healing and Equipping". https://houseofhealingandequipping.org

YOUNG CO-AUTHORS

This book could not have been written without the contribution and inspiration of Emery, Harper and Paisley. May they continue expressing their own creative legacies.

ABOUT THE ILLUSTRATOR

Madelyn Graham demonstrated artistic expressions since first holding a pencil. This first book is her dream come true. She is majoring in Illustration at the Art Academy of Cincinnati. Her career goal is to continue illustrating children's books and graphic novels.

Examples are on Instagram

@drawing_with_madz